LAUBACH WAY TO READING

SKILL BOOK 3

LONG VOWEL SOUNDS

Use with the following Teacher's Manual(s):

For English-speaking students

- Laubach Way to Reading: *Teacher's Manual for Skill Book 3*

For speakers of other languages

- Laubach Way to Reading: *Teacher's Manual for Skill Book 3* (for reading and writing)

- Laubach Way to English: *ESOL Teacher's Manual for Skill Book 3* (for listening and speaking)

Frank C. Laubach

Elizabeth Mooney Kirk

Robert S. Laubach

Linguistic Consultant:
Jeanette D. Macero

ISBN 0-88336-903-6

© 1982, 1991

New Readers Press
Publishing Division of
Laubach Literacy
1320 Jamesville Ave., Syracuse, New York 13210

Printed in the United States of America

Edited by Caroline Blakely and Kay Koschnick

Illustrated by Cheri Bladholm

20 19 18 17 16 15

Lesson 1

vowels ✓

ā, ē, ī, ō, ū, ȳ, (ī)

	paper	p ā p er ā	paper
	we	w ē ē	we
	I	ī ī	I
	go	g ō ō	go
	music	m ū z i c ū	music
	my	m ȳ ȳ (ī)	my

or

York St.	York	Y or k or	York

My Class

Jason (Jāson)	Carla (Carlu)	class	listen	(lisen)
David (Dāvid)	Lopez (Lōpez)	snack	write	(rīt)
		study	sentence	(sentens)

I am Jason Hunt. I work at a market on River Street. I go to class after work. I have some paper. The paper is for my class.

After work, I will pick up my friend David Miller. He works at a factory on York Street. I will pick up David at the factory. We will go to class in my car.

Carla Lopez works at a music shop on York Street. We will pick up Carla at the music shop. She will go to class with us.

We will study hard in class. We will study the lesson. We will write on the paper. We will write sentences. We will write letters to friends. Ms. Smith will help us write sentences. She will help us write letters.

After class, Carla, David, and I will go for a snack. We will go to Fran's Snack Shop. It is on York Street. We can get a quick snack at Fran's. We can listen to music. We can have a snack and listen to music.

From the snack shop, we will go to Garden Street. Carla lives on Garden Street. Then David and I will go to First Street. David lives at 917 First Street. I live at 942 First Street.

I work hard. I study hard. But I have fun.

Story Checkup

The names in this story are:

Jason Hunt   David Miller   Carla Lopez   Ms. Smith

Write the name.

1. Who works at the market? _____

2. Who works at the factory? _____

3. Who works at the music shop? _____

4. Who has a car?_____

5. Who lives on Garden Street? _____

6. Who lives on First Street?

    _____ and _____

7. Who will go to class with Jason?

    _____ and _____

8. Who will help them write? _____

Write the missing word.

live
lives   1. David and Jason _____ on First Street.

work
works   2. I _____ at the market.

work
works   3. Carla _____ at a music shop.

write
writes   4. We _____ on the paper.

read (rēd)

ham	milk	I'll (Īll)	salad (salud)
hamburger	drink	sandwich	coffee (coffē)

Jason, Carla, and David were in Fran's Snack Shop.
Fran hurried to them.

Fran asked, "What will you have?"

Jason said, "I'll have a ham sandwich."
Carla said, "I'll have an egg salad sandwich."
David said, "I'll have a hamburger."

Fran asked Jason, "What will you have to drink?"
Jason said, "I'll have a glass of milk."

Fran asked Carla, "What will you have to drink?"
Carla said, "I'll have a cup of coffee."

Fran asked David, "What will you have to drink?"
David said, "I'll have a glass of milk."

bill	¢ (cent)	75¢	(seventy-five cents)
cost	$ (dollar)	$1.00	(one dollar)
		$1.50	(one dollar and fifty cents)

Sandwiches

Ham sandwich $2.50
Egg salad sandwich. . . $1.50
Hamburger $2.25

Drinks

Milk . . . . 75¢
Coffee . . . . 50¢

Write the missing numbers with $ or ¢.

Jason got a ham sandwich.

The ham sandwich cost _____.

Jason got a glass of milk.

The milk cost _____.

His bill was $3.25.

Carla got an egg salad sandwich.

The egg salad sandwich cost _____.

Carla got a cup of coffee.

The coffee cost _____.

Her bill was $2.00.

David got a hamburger.

The hamburger cost _____.

David got a glass of milk.

The milk cost _____.

His bill was $3.00.

Copy the word. Add -s or -es. What is the word?

egg _eggs_   dish _dishes_

1. glass _____
2. car _____
3. drink _____
4. class _____
5. dress _____

6. paper _____
7. salad _____
8. box _____
9. friend _____
10. sandwich _____

Drop -s or -es. Write the word.

friends _friend_   dishes _dish_

1. cups _____
2. bills _____
3. classes _____
4. words _____
5. glasses _____

6. sentences _____
7. names _____
8. kisses _____
9. sandwiches _____
10. shops _____

ā

paper

ā

	David	Dā vid	David
	April	Ā pril	April
	baby	bā by	baby
	lady	lā dy	lady
	table	tā bul	table
	radio	rā dē ō	radio

Carla's Story

love (luv)	me (mē)	apartment (u part ment)
month (munth)	Rosa (Rō su)	baby-sitter (ba bē sit er)

My name is Carla Lopez. I live in an apartment on Garden Street. I have lived in this apartment for ten months.

I work at a music shop. I started work in April. I have worked at the music shop for six months.

After work, I go to class. I started the class in April. April was not a bad month! David was at the first class. David has helped me a lot in class. He and I are friends. David helps me with Rosa. He loves Rosa.

Rosa is my baby. She is two. My baby cannot go to work with me. She cannot go to class with me. A baby-sitter must look after her. Mrs. King is my baby-sitter. Mrs. King is a lady in my apartment building. This lady loves my baby. My baby loves her. I am happy that this lady is my baby-sitter.

It is after work. I have picked up Rosa from Mrs. King's apartment. Rosa is with me in the kitchen. Rosa is sitting at the table. She is singing. I am working at the table. I am starting dinner.

A radio is on the table. I am listening to the radio. The radio says that it is half past six. I must hurry. My friend David is coming to dinner.

Answer with one or two words. Write the answer.

1. Who has worked at the music shop for six months?

_____

2. Who has helped Carla in class? _____

3. When did Carla start the class? _____

4. Who is the baby-sitter? _____

5. What is the baby's name? _____

6. Who is coming to dinner? _____

Answer with yes or no. Write the answer.

1. Does Carla Lopez live on Garden Street? _____

2. Is David Carla's brother? _____

3. Can Rosa go to class with Carla? _____

4. Does Rosa love the baby-sitter? _____

5. Did Carla pick up Rosa after work? _____

6. Is Carla listening to the radio? _____

instant (in stant)   potatoes (pu tā tōz)   pat   water (wot er)

Carla is getting dinner. She and David will have ham, salad, and potatoes for dinner. The potatoes are instant potatoes. This is on the box of instant potatoes.

	Water	Butter	Milk	Instant Potatoes
For 1 person	1 half cup	1 pat	1 quarter cup	1 half cup
For 2 persons	1 cup	2 pats	1 half cup	1 cup
For 4 persons	2 cups	4 pats	1 cup	2 cups

Put water, butter, and milk in a pan.
When the water gets hot, add instant potatoes.
Cover and let stand.

Fill in the numbers and words.

1. Carla is getting dinner for two persons.

   She puts _____ of water in a pan.

   She puts in _____ of butter.

   She puts in _____ of milk.

   When the water gets hot, she adds _____ of instant potatoes.

2. I have four persons in my family. For four persons,

   I will put _____ of water in a pan.

   I will put in _____ of butter.

   I will put in _____ of milk.

   When the water gets hot, I will add _____ of instant potatoes.

practice (prac tis), say (sā), sound, syllable (sil u bul)

Say the words. Which word has the sound ā? Circle that word.

snack   (snake)

1. baby   happy   5. after   April
2. apple   table   6. Jason   happen
3. paper   faster   7. Dan   David
4. name   man   8. radio   traffic

Look at the picture, and say the word.
Under the picture, write the number of syllables in the word.

1. _____   2. _____   3. _____   4. _____

5. _____   6. _____   7. _____   8. _____

Write the word.

baby
mother   1. Rosa is Carla's _____.

man
woman   2. The baby-sitter is a _____.

six
ten   3. The radio says it is half past _____.

David
Jason   4. _____ is coming to dinner.

ham
fish   5. They will have _____ for dinner.

Say the word. Write the number of syllables.

1. lady   _2_   7. has   _____

2. hat   _____   8. radio   _____

3. April   _____   9. paper   _____

4. potato   _____   10. apartment   _____

5. that   _____   11. man   _____

6. baby   _____   12. hamburger   _____

ay = ā

day = dā

ay = ā

	pay	pay	pay
May	May	May	May
	Kay	Kay	Kay
	Ray	Ray	Ray
	play	play	play
	away	u way	away

After Payday

rent	next	card	Mason	(Mā son)	today	(to day)
spent	last	check	hundred	(hun dred)	yesterday	(yes ter day)
had					payday	(pay day)

Today is the first day of May. Yesterday was payday. Yesterday was payday for Kay and Ray Mason. Their payday is the last day of the month. They got six hundred dollars.

The Masons are paying their bills today. Ray is looking at the bills. Kay is writing checks.

The Masons have to pay a lot of bills in May. They have to pay their rent today. The rent is for May. They have to pay the telephone bill for April. They have to pay the water bill for three months. They have to pay Kay's doctor bill. They have to pay some other bills.

Kay writes a check for the rent. She writes checks for the other bills.

Ray asks, "Have we spent the last cent?"

Kay laughs, "No, we have not spent the last cent. But we have spent a lot. Yesterday, we had six hundred twenty-five dollars. Today, we have seventy-five dollars left."

"We can live on that," Ray says. "The next payday is May 15. But can we have any fun?"

Kay says, "Yes, we can play cards. Carla and David can come and play cards with us. It is fun to play cards."

Ray says, "We can have a little fun. But we can have a lot of fun after the next payday. We will have six hundred dollars. And we will not have many bills then. We can go away after the next payday. Let's go away the last three days in May."

"Yes, let's go away then," says Kay.

Story Checkup

Write a short *yes* or *no* answer.

Was yesterday the Masons' payday ?   <u>Yes, it was.</u>

1. Do the Masons have to pay a lot of bills? _____

2. Does Ray write the checks? _____

3. Have the Masons spent a lot? _____

4. Have they spent their last cent? _____

5. Is their next payday April 15? _____

6. Can the Masons play cards? _____

7. Do the Masons plan to go away in May? _____

bank   your

On April 29, the Masons had $25.00 in the bank. On April 30, they put $600.00 in the bank. Then they had $625.00 in the bank. They had to pay their bills with that $625.00.

Today is May 1. Kay writes a check for the rent. This is the check.

	301
Ray Mason	
Kay Mason	May 1 19 96
Pay to __Ellen Smith__	$ 275.00
Two hundred seventy-five and 00/100 ~~ DOLLARS	
First City Bank	
Garden City, CA	Kay Mason

Today is May 15. You are paying your bills. You have a bill from Dr. John Black. The bill is for $75.00. Write the check to pay your bill. Write your name on the check.

	1264
	_____ 19___
Pay to _____	$ _____
_____ DOLLARS	
_____	

Say the words. Which word has the sound ā? Circle that word.

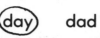 (day)   dad

1.	ran	Ray	5.	Pam	pay
2.	play	plan	6.	Kay	Cal
3.	any	away	7.	say	Sam
4.	May	many	8.	valley	today

Copy the word. Add -ing.
Then write the words in the sentences.

pick _____ picking _____

Carla is _____ picking _____ up Rosa.

play _____   go _____

pay _____   start _____

1. I am _____ to class.

2. Carla is _____ dinner.

3. The Masons are _____ their bills.

4. Kay and Ray are _____ cards.

Write the missing word.

1. Yesterday was _____ for the Masons.

2. They got six _____ dollars.

3. The Masons are _____ their bills.

4. Kay is writing _____.

5. They have _____ dollars left.

6. The next payday is _____ 15.

Say the word. Write the number of syllables.

1. pay   _____
2. paying   _____
3. go   _____
4. play   _____
5. yesterday   _____
6. today   _____
7. rent   _____

8. hundred   _____
9. next   _____
10. playing   _____
11. cards   _____
12. going   _____
13. telephone   _____
14. day   _____

$$ai = \bar{a}$$

paint = pānt

ai = ā

	nail	nail	nail
	Gail	Gail	Gail
	paid	paid	paid
	hair	hair	hair
	chair	chair	chair
	stairs	stairz	stairs

Painting

shall	ever (ev er)	OK	(ō kay)
gray	never (nev er)	landlady (land lady)	

Gail Fisher and Jason Hunt planned to get married. They rented an apartment. They said to the landlady, "We will paint the kitchen. Will you pay for the paint?"

The landlady asked, "Have you ever painted a kitchen?"

Jason said, "No, I have never painted a kitchen. But I have painted stairs."

"OK," said the landlady. "You get the paint and some nails. You can fix the stairs first. Then you can paint the stairs and your kitchen. I'll pay you for the paint and the nails."

"Shall we paint the kitchen red?" asked Jason.

"No, let's not," said Gail. "Let's paint it pink. What color shall we paint the stairs?"

Jason said, "Let's paint the stairs gray. Shall we get some black paint? We can paint the table and chairs black."

"OK," said Gail.

Jason and Gail got the paint and the nails. Gail paid for them.

The landlady paid Gail for the pink and gray paint. She paid Gail for the nails.

Gail and Jason got ready to paint. Gail covered her hair.

"Have you ever had paint in your hair?" Jason asked.

Gail said, "No, I never have. I cover my hair when I paint. Shall we paint the table and chairs first?"

Jason said, "No, let's not. Let's paint the kitchen first. Then you can paint the table and chairs. I have never painted chairs. I'll fix the stairs and paint them."

Story Checkup

Write a short *yes* or *no* answer.

Has Jason ever painted a kitchen?   _No, he has not._

1. Have Gail and Jason rented an apartment? _____

2. Will they paint the kitchen red? _____

3. Has Jason ever painted chairs? _____

4. Did Gail cover her hair? _____

5. Did the landlady pay for the gray paint? _____

6. Did the landlady pay for the black paint? _____

7. Will Jason paint the table and chairs? _____

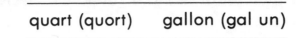

quart (quort)   gallon (gal un)

Pink Paint

$7 a quart
$21 a gallon

Gray Paint

$8 a quart
$24 a gallon

Black Paint

$10 a quart
$30 a gallon

Write the missing number with $.

1. Gail and Jason got one gallon of pink paint.

   They paid _____ for it.

2. They got one gallon of gray paint.

   They paid _____ for it.

3. They got two quarts of black paint.

   They paid _____ for it.

4. The pink, gray, and black paint cost _____.

5. Their landlady paid them for the pink and gray paint.

   She paid them _____.

Say the words. Which word has the sound ā? Circle that word.

1. paint   pan   5. chair   Chan
2. starts   stairs   6. neck   nail
3. Gail   girl   7. hair   has
4. pack   paid   8. gray   grass

Copy the word. Add -ed.
Then write the words in the sentences.

play __played__

They _____played_____ cards.

paint _____   ask _____

rent _____   cover _____

1. Jason and Gail _____ an apartment.

2. Jason has never _____ a kitchen.

3. Gail _____ her hair.

4. "Shall we paint the kitchen red?" _____ Jason.

Answer with a sentence.

1. What did Gail and Jason rent? _____

_____

2. What color will they paint the kitchen?_____

_____

3. Who will paint the stairs? _____

_____

4. Who will paint the chairs? _____

_____

Say the word. Write the number of syllables.

1. paint _____   6. asked _____

2. painted _____   7. covered _____

3. stairs _____   8. landlady _____

4. chairs _____   9. paid _____

5. rented _____   10. never _____

$a-e=\bar{a}$

cake = cāk

a – e = ā

	bake	bake bāk	bake
	take	take tāk	take
	Jane	Jane Jăn	Jane
	ate	ate ăt	ate
	plate	plate plăt	plate
	care	care căr	care

The Wedding

yet	came	where (whare)	church	wedding (wed ing)
still	gave	there (thare)	party (par ty)	yourself (your self)

Jason and Gail got married in Gail's church. Jason's family and friends came to the wedding. Gail's family and friends came. After the wedding, there was a party. The party was in a building next to the church.

At the party, there was a big wedding cake. It was on a pretty glass plate. There were little sandwiches, coffee, and other drinks. There were paper plates and cups.

"Take a plate and help yourself to sandwiches," said Gail's sister Jane. "And help yourself to drinks."

"May I have some cake?" asked Jason's little brother Sam.

"No, not yet," said Jane. "Jason and Gail have to cut the cake first."

"Where are they?" asked Sam.

"They are still in the church," Jane said. "Gail's uncle is still taking pictures of them. He will take a picture of the wedding cake when they cut it."

"Who baked the wedding cake?" asked Carla.

Jane said, "Jason's mother baked it. She bakes many wedding cakes."

Just then, Jason and Gail came from the church. They cut the wedding cake. Jason gave Gail some cake, and she gave him some. They ate their cake.

Jason's little brother said, "I have not had any cake yet." Jason gave him some.

Gail said to the others, "Come and help yourself to some cake." Their family ate cake. Their friends ate cake.

Jason said to Gail, "Let's go!"

Jason's little brother said, "Where are you going?"

"Away," Jason said.

"You cannot go yet," said Gail's father. "I still have not kissed my little girl." He kissed Gail and said, "Take care of her, Jason."

Jason said, "Yes, Dad, I will take care of her. And she will take care of me."

Story Checkup

right (rīt)

Circle the letter of the right answer.

Who got married?
(a.) Jason and Gail
b. Carla and David

1. Where was the wedding?
   a. in Gail's church
   b. in Carla's apartment

2. Where was the party?
   a. in the church
   b. in a building next to the church

3. Where was the wedding cake?
   a. on a paper plate
   b. on a glass plate

4. Who was taking pictures?
   a. Gail's father
   b. Gail's uncle

frame	much
date	dear (dēr)

Gail and Jason got many wedding gifts. Some of the gifts were glasses, plates, curtains, a chair, a table, a rug, a clock radio, and a picture frame.

Gail is writing thank you letters for the gifts. First, she writes the date. She puts the date at the top of the letter. She starts the letter with the word *Dear* and the person's name.

May 21, 1995

Dear Carla,

Thank you very much for the picture frame. Jason and I think that it is very pretty. We will put a wedding picture in the frame.

Thank you very much for coming to the wedding. You are a dear friend.

With love,
Gail

1. What is the date on the letter? _____

2. Who is the letter to?_____

3. What was the gift? _____

4. Who is Gail's dear friend? _____

Practice

Say the words. Circle the words with the sound ā.

(bake) back (gave) bank

1. came cake gave bank

2. gray Gail girl care

3. check chair hair Chan

4. Sam Ray Jane Ann

5. ham plate play class

Copy the word but not the e. Add -ing.
Then write the words in the sentences.

have _havíng_____

They are _____havíng_____ a party.

take _____   give _____

bake _____   write _____

1. Jason's mother is _____ a cake.

2. Gail's uncle is _____ pictures.

3. Gail is _____ a letter.

4. Jane is _____ Sam some cake.

Answer with a sentence.

1. Where was the wedding? _____

_____

2. Who baked the wedding cake? _____

_____

3. Who cut the wedding cake? _____

_____

4. Who gave Sam some cake? _____

_____

Say the word. Write the number of syllables.

1. baked	_____	6. much	_____
2. wedding	_____	7. taking	_____
3. yourself	_____	8. baking	_____
4. came	_____	9. party	_____
5. kissed	_____	10. writing	_____

More Reading with ā

paper	cake	paint	day
ā	a–e	ai	ay

1. Dinner for Two

TV

David came to Carla's apartment for dinner. When he came in, he kissed Carla. He said, "Your hair looks very pretty."

"Thank you, dear," said Carla. "My landlady cut my hair yesterday."

"Where is Rosa?" asked David.

"She is in bed," Carla said. "Dinner is ready. Help yourself to coffee, and I'll drink milk."

David and Carla ate their dinner. They had ham, potatoes, and salad.

After dinner, they had coffee and watched TV.

2. The Card Party

Carla and David came to the Masons' apartment. They came to play cards. They did not bring Carla's baby with them. The baby-sitter was taking care of her.

Ray Mason put four chairs at the card table. The friends played cards and listened to music on the radio. After they played cards, they ate some cake. They had coffee with their cake.

"Kay, did you bake this cake?" asked David.

"No," said Kay. "Ray baked it today."

"Your plates are very pretty," Carla said.

"Thank you very much," said Kay. "My mother gave them to me."

After they ate their cake, David and Carla thanked the Masons and left.

3. Three Days at Snake River

The Masons' payday was May 15. They put their checks in the bank and paid their bills. They went away for the last three days in May.

Kay and Ray went to Snake River. They had fun there. They fished in the river. They played in the water. They picked up pretty rocks.

When they came back, Ray said, "We spent a hundred dollars. But it was fun."

4. In the Kitchen

It was a month after the Hunts' wedding. Gail and Jason were sitting in their kitchen. They were having a snack. There were some sandwiches and a quart of milk on the table.

The landlady came up the stairs. Jason said, "Come in and have a snack with us."

"No, thanks," she said. "But may I look at your kitchen? I am happy that you painted it pink. I have a gallon of paint. Will you paint my kitchen? I will pay you for it."

"OK," said Jason. "We will paint it next month."

we
ē

ē

ee = ē

see = sē
ee = ē

	he	hē	he
	tree	tree	tree
	wheel	wheel	wheel
	teeth	teeth	teeth
	sleep	sleep	sleep

Lee's Lesson

Lee	need	be	late	again (u gen)	wasn't (wuz unt)
Green	beer	it's	face (fase)	angry (ang gry)	didn't (did unt)

Mrs. Green was in bed, but she wasn't sleeping. "Where is Lee?" she was thinking. "It's half past three."

Lee was 16. He had a job after class. He had his first car.

Mrs. Green heard a car. When Lee came in, she got up. "Where were you?" she yelled. "It's half past three. Were you drinking beer?"

"No, Mother," said Lee. "I wasn't drinking beer. I was just playing cards with my friends."

Mrs. Green said, "I cannot sleep when you come in late. You need to be in bed. You need your sleep."

"OK," said Lee. "Let's go to bed."

"What is that?" his mother said. "Do I see a cut on your face? Yes, I *do* see a cut."

"It's just a little cut," Lee said. "I went to sleep at the wheel. I didn't see the tree. My car hit the tree. My face hit the wheel. But I wasn't going fast. And I wasn't drinking beer!"

Mrs. Green said, "Did you hit your teeth on the wheel?"

"No, I didn't hit my teeth," Lee said. "My teeth are OK, and my face will be OK. My car still runs, but the tree looks bad."

Lee said, "Do not be angry with me, Mother. I have had a hard lesson. I will not be late again."

"I was very angry," said Mrs. Green. "And I am still angry. Do not be late again, or I will take your car away."

"But, Mother, I need my car to go to work," said Lee.

"Then do not be late again," she said. "And you will have to pay for that tree."

Story Checkup

Circle the letter of the right answer.

1. Did Lee have a car?
   a. Yes, he had a car.
   b. No, he didn't have a car.

2. Was Mrs. Green sleeping?
   a. Yes, she was sleeping.
   b. No, she wasn't sleeping.

3. Did Lee hit his teeth?
   a. Yes, he hit his teeth.
   b. No, he didn't hit his teeth.

4. Was Mrs. Green angry?
   a. Yes, she was angry.
   b. No, she wasn't angry.

5. Is Lee's face cut?
   a. Yes, it's cut a little.
   b. No, it's not cut.

1 one	11 eleven (ē lev en)	10 ten
2 two	12 twelve	20 twenty
3 three	13 thirteen	30 thirty
4 four	14 fourteen	40 forty
5 five	15 fifteen	50 fifty
6 six	16 sixteen	60 sixty
7 seven	17 seventeen	70 seventy
8 eight (āt)	18 eighteen	80 eighty
9 nine (nīn)	19 nineteen	90 ninety
10 ten	20 twenty	100 one hundred

Write the number.

nine	9	thirteen	13	seventy-seven	77
nineteen	___	thirty	___	ninety-nine	___
ninety	___	fifteen	___	sixty-six	___
eight	___	fifty	___	eighty-eight	___
eighteen	___	fourteen	___	fifty-five	___
eighty	___	forty	___	forty-four	___
eleven	___	sixteen	___	thirty-three	___
seven	___	sixty	___	thirteen	___
seventeen	___	eleven	___	fifteen	___

Say the words. Which word has the sound ē? Circle that word.

1.	Ned	need	5.	bed	beer
2.	well	wheel	6.	teeth	tent
3.	see	send	7.	sleep	seven
4.	Lee	let	8.	ten	teen

Say the word. Write the two words that it comes from.

let's   <u>let</u>   <u>us</u>

1. it's   _____   _____

2. wasn't   _____   _____

3. didn't   _____   _____

4. I'll   _____   _____

Fill in the word: *let's, it's, wasn't, didn't, I'll.*

1. _____ not a bad cut.

2. Lee _____ see the tree.

3. He _____ drinking beer

4. _____ pay you for the paint.

5. _____ not go to the party.

Answer with a sentence.

1. Who was angry? _____

_____

2. Who went to sleep at the wheel? _____

_____

3. What did Lee's car hit? _____

_____

4. Who will have to pay for the tree? _____

_____

Say the word. Write the number of syllables.

1. seventeen _____   6. fifty _____

2. nineteen _____   7. drinking _____

3. nine _____   8. yelled _____

4. fourteen _____   9. better _____

5. sleeping _____   10. need _____

$$ea = \bar{e}$$

eat = $\bar{e}$t

ea = $\bar{e}$

	meat	meat	meat
	meal	meal	meal
	beans	beanz	beans
	tea	tea	tea
	teacher	teach er	teacher
	please	pleaz	please

The Class Party

each	eaten (eat en)	cheese (cheez)	best
cheap		people (pē pul)	something (some thing)

Carla's class is having a dinner party. There will be a big meal.

Each person brings something to eat. Carla brings beans. David brings a green salad. Jason and Gail bring baked potatoes. The Masons bring apples and cheese. Other people bring something to eat.

Ms. Smith, the teacher, brings the meat. The meat wasn't cheap. Each person helped to pay for the meat.

There are eighteen people at the party. They are having fun and eating a big meal.

"Please pass the meat," says Ray. "I have not eaten any meat for three days."

Kay says, "That is right. Meat is not cheap. For many meals, we have eggs, beans, or cheese. They are pretty cheap."

The teacher says, "Please pass the beans. Carla's beans are the best beans that I have ever eaten."

Jason says, "This is the best salad that I have ever eaten."

The people at the party eat their dinner. Then Ray passes apples and cheese. The teacher brings coffee and tea to the table. She asks each person, "Will you have coffee or tea?"

"I'll have tea, please," says Gail. "And Jason will have coffee."

"This is the best party that we have ever had," says Carla. "Let's have another one."

Story Checkup

Write a short answer.

1. Who is having a party? _____

2. What does Carla bring? _____

3. What do Jason and Gail bring? _____

4. Who brings the meat? _____

5. Who pays for the meat? _____

Read this list of words.
Then write one of the words in each sentence.

eat, meal, tea, please, cheap

1. The people are eating a big _____.

2. Each person brings something to _____.

3. _____ pass the meat.

4. Will you have coffee or _____ ?

5. The meat wasn't _____.

ad

Please read this ad. Then write the answers.

1. Hamburger is in the ad. What other meat is there?_____

2. What three things to drink are in this ad?

_____

3. What does a quart of milk cost?_____

4. What does a half gallon of milk cost? _____

5. What does the bread cost? _____

6. What does a box of 100 tea bags cost? _____

7. What do two cans of green beans cost?_____

8. What does a jar of instant coffee cost? _____

Practice

Say the words. Which word has the sound ē? Circle the word.

1. it   eat
2. tea   ten
3. dark   dear
4. red   read

5. meat   men
6. plate   please
7. bill   meal
8. bean   best

Copy the word. Add -r or -er.
Then write one of the words in each sentence.

farm _farmer_

Mr. Arthur is a _farmer_ .

write _writer_

Ann is a _writer_ .

teach _____

paint _____

bake _____

read _____

1. Ms. Smith is Carla's _____.

2. The _____ is painting the apartment.

3. The _____ is baking bread.

4. She can read the story quickly.

   She is a fast _____.

Answer with a sentence.

1. What do the Masons bring? _____

   _____

2. Who brings a salad? _____

   _____

3. What does Ms. Smith bring to the table? _____

   _____

   _____

Say the word. Write the number of syllables.

1. tea _____   7. baking _____

2. people _____   8. baker _____

3. eat _____   9. read _____

4. something _____   10. reader _____

5. eaten _____   11. teacher _____

6. baked _____   12. potatoes _____

Pete = Pēt

e-e = ē

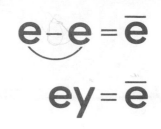

e-e = ē

ey = ē

key = kē

ey = ē

	Steve	St<u>eve</u>	Steve
	these	th<u>eze</u>	these
	evening	<u>eve</u> ning	evening
	valley	val ey	valley
	money	mun ey	money

Steve's Job

clean	keep	make	repair (rē pair)
teach	week	save	Saturday (Sat ur day)
	here	place (plase)	

Steve is seventeen. He has a job at Pete's Valley Repair Shop. Pete repairs radios, TVs, and other things.

Steve's job is to keep the place clean. He keeps the shop clean. He keeps the stairs clean. Pete is teaching him to repair radios. Next, Pete will teach him to repair TVs.

Steve works from six to nine in the evening. And he works on Saturday.

Steve does not make much money at his job. He makes $90 a week. Steve saves some of his money. He has worked at the repair shop for six weeks. In six weeks, he has saved $120 dollars. He is saving his money to get a color TV.

One evening, Pete gives Steve some keys. "These are the keys to the shop," Pete says. "I will not be here on Saturday. You can take care of the place."

"OK," says Steve. "I will be here at eight on Saturday. I will take care of the place very well."

Pete says, "A lot of people will come in to pick up their things. These radios are ready. These TVs are ready. I was going to repair Mrs. Green's radio yesterday, but I didn't. You can fix it."

On Saturday, Mrs. Green comes in. Steve gives her the radio that he fixed. Other people come in. Steve gives them their things and takes their money.

That evening, Pete comes back. Steve says, "Here are your keys. Here is the money that I got today. I fixed Mrs. Green's radio, and she picked it up."

Pete says, "You can keep the money she gave you. You worked hard today."

Story Checkup

Write a short yes or no answer.

1. Is Steve fifteen? _____

2. Has Steve saved $120? _____

3. Did Pete work in the shop on Saturday? _____

4. Did Steve repair Mrs. Green's radio? _____

5. Is Pete teaching Steve to repair radios? _____

Read these five sentences. What happened first?
You will see a number 1 next to that sentence.
What happened next? Put a number 2 next to that sentence.
Put the right numbers next to the other sentences.

_____ Steve fixes Mrs. Green's radio.

___1___ Pete gives Steve some keys.

_____ Steve gives Mrs. Green the radio.

_____ Steve gives Pete the keys.

_____ That evening, Pete comes back.

second (sec und)   tax   labor (lā ber)
third   part

PETE'S VALLEY REPAIR SHOP
332 Second Street
Garden City

Name _Jane Fisher_

Address _332 Third Street_

Date _April 16, 1994_
For TV repair

Parts	$23.13
Labor	40.00
Subtotal	63.13
Tax	4.42
Total	$67.55

Please read this bill. Then write short answers.

1. What is this bill for? _____

2. What do the parts cost? $ _____

3. What does the labor cost? $ _____

4. What is the tax? $ _____

5. Which costs more, the parts or the labor? _____

6. Which costs more, the parts or the tax? _____

7. What does Jane Fisher have to pay? $ _____

8. What is the date on the bill? _____

9. Is the repair shop on Second Street? _____

10. Does Jane Fisher live on Third Street? _____

Say the words. Circle the words with the sound ē.

1. clean   class   please   last
2. money   meat   key   month
3. well   week   went   with
4. these   here   her   this
5. pet   Pete   teach   pick

Drop *-ing* or *-ed*. Write the word that is left.

1. keeping _____

2. painted _____

3. eating _____

4. played _____

5. drinking _____

6. reading _____

7. repaired _____

8. needed _____

9. paying _____

10. yelled _____

11. cleaned _____

12. teaching _____

Answer with a sentence.

1. Where does Steve work? _____

_____

2. What is Steve saving his money for? _____

_____

3. Who repaired Mrs. Green's radio? _____

_____

4. Who gave the keys to Steve? _____

_____

Say the word. Write the number of syllables.

1. cleaned _____   6. Saturday _____

2. repaired _____   7. week _____

3. money _____   8. yesterday _____

4. saved _____   9. fixed _____

5. seventeen _____   10. labor _____

Lesson 10

More Reading with ā and ē

paper ā	cake a–e	paint ai		day ay
we ē	Pete e–e	eat ea	see ee	key ey

1. A Teenager Pays

teenager (teen āj er)

It was Saturday. Lee Green went to see the tree that he hit. When he got there, a woman was standing next to the tree. She looked angry. "Are you the teenager that hit my tree?" she asked.

"Yes, I am," said Lee. "I went to sleep at the wheel."

"You teenagers!" she yelled, and her face got red. "You do not care what you do! You drink beer! You go fast in your cars! You do not need cars!"

"I am a teenager," said Lee. "But I wasn't drinking beer. I wasn't going fast. And I do care. I came to pay for your tree."

"We cannot save this tree," said the woman. "It will not live. It will cost a hundred dollars to get another one."

"That is a lot of money," said Lee. "I can pay you twenty dollars today. I have a job. I can pay you twenty dollars a week."

The woman said, "I am happy that you came back. You are OK."

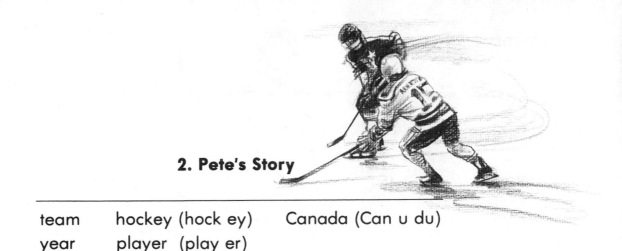

2. Pete's Story

team	hockey (hock ey)	Canada (Can u du)
year	player (play er)	

I am Pete. I run the repair shop on Second Street. Steve works for me in the evenings. He keeps the place clean. I am teaching him to repair things.

Let me tell you my story. I was a teenager in the 1950s. I lived with my mother in Canada. My father was dead. When I was nineteen, I got a job with a hockey team in Canada. I was going to be a big hockey player and make a lot of money.

My mother left Canada and came back to Garden City. Then she got sick. She needed me to take care of her. I came to Garden City. I got a job at a TV factory. I started repairing TVs. I repaired them in the evening at the kitchen table.

Many years passed. My mother did not get well. I never went back to my hockey team. After fourteen years, I started my repair shop.

When I think back, I am not very happy. I was going to be a big hockey player. Many people were going to see me play. I was going to make a lot of money. These things never happened.

But I am happy with the hockey team that I have today. There are fifteen teenagers on my team. I am teaching these boys to play hockey. They think that I am the best hockey player there is.

"Not the best," I tell them. "But I still have my teeth, and a lot of hockey players do not. And I have you. We will be the best hockey team in the valley. And next year we will play in Canada."

I
i

$\bar{\text{I}}$

$\text{i} - \text{e} = \bar{\text{I}}$

  time

$\text{i} - \text{e} = \bar{\text{I}}$

	ride	$r\bar{\text{i}}de$ $r\bar{\text{i}}d$	ride
	drive	$dr\bar{\text{i}}ve$ $dr\bar{\text{i}}v$	drive
	driver	$dr\bar{\text{i}}v$ er	driver
	license	$l\bar{\text{i}}$ sens	license
	bicycle	$b\bar{\text{i}}$ sic ul	bicycle

Getting a Driver's License

| eye (ī) | same | test | written (rit en) |
| if | state | tester (test er) | permit (per mit) |

Who needs a driver's license? What do I have to do to get one? Do I need license plates? The answers are not the same in each of the 50 states. But the answers are the same in many states.

You need a license to drive a car. You need a license to drive a truck. You do not need a license to ride a bicycle.

You must have license plates for your car. You must have license plates for a truck. In some places, you have to have license plates for a bicycle. In other places, you do not have to have license plates for a bicycle.

You get license plates from the state that you live in. You get your driver's license from your state.

To get a driver's license, you must take tests. One test is an eye test. To take this test, you have to read letters on a chart. The eye test tells if you need glasses to drive.

Another test is a written test. If you do not pass the written test the first time, you must not drive. But you can take this test again.

If you pass the written test, you get a permit to drive. A permit is not a license. But with a permit, you can start driving. Another person must ride with you. That person must have a driver's license.

The last test is a driving test. You are ready to take it when you can drive well. A tester will ride with you. The tester tells you where to drive and when to turn. The tester watches your driving and parking.

If you pass the driving test, you will get a driver's license. Many people do not pass this test the first time. If you do not pass the first time, you can take the driving test again. You can take it again and again.

Story Checkup

Circle yes or no.

1. Do you need a license to ride a bicycle?   Yes   No

2. Do you have to take tests to get a
   driver's license?   Yes   No

3. If you do not pass the written test, can
   you take it again?   Yes   No

4. Do you have to take an eye test to get
   a driver's license?   Yes   No

5. Do you have to take a test to get
   license plates?   Yes   No

6. Is a permit a license?   Yes   No

7. Can you take the driving test two times?   Yes   No

8. Do you have a driver's license?   Yes   No

birth	Dallas (Dal us)	zip code	(cōd)
sex	Texas (Tex us)	application (ap li cā shun)	

State of Texas
Application for Driver's License

_____Baker_____   _____Ann_____
Last name   First name

Date of birth: _May 9, 1962_   Sex: ☐ M ☒ F   Eye color: _Green_
                Month/Day/Year

Address: __3214 Church Street__
          Number and Street

__Dallas__   __Texas__   __75203__
City   State   Zip code

**This is part of an application for a driver's license.
Read the application, and write short answers.**

1. What is this person's first name? _____

2. What is this person's last name? _____

3. Which box did this person mark for Sex? _____

4. Is this person a man or a woman? _____

5. What is her date of birth? _____

6. What is her street address in Dallas? _____

7. Is Texas a city or a state? _____

8. What is Ann's zip code? _____

9. What is your sex? Put an X in one box.   ☐ M   ☐ F

10. What is the year of your birth? _____

Say the words. Circle the words with the sound ī.

1. ride   drive   ring   sick
2. I   if   eye   first
3. driving   living   driver   river
4. fit   time   license   with
5. building   bicycle   written   write

Copy the word. Add -r or -er.
Then write one of the words in each sentence.

ride _____   drive _____

test _____   play _____

1. A bicycle _____ does not need a license.

2. The _____ will ride with you when you take
   the driving test.

3. The _____ of a car must have a license.

4. Pete is a hockey _____.

Write short answers.

1. What is your first name? _____

2. What is your last name? _____

3. What is your street address?

    _____

4. What is the name of your state? _____

5. What is your zip code? _____

6. Do you have a driver's license? _____

Say the word. Write the number of syllables.

1. driver _____   6. license _____

2. bicycle _____   7. state _____

3. written _____   8. letters _____

4. tester _____   9. glasses _____

5. ride _____   10. application _____

i − e = ī

time

i − e = ī

	Mike	Mike / Mīk	Mike
	like	like / līk	like
MILE 4 4	mile	mile / mīl	mile
	smile	smile / smīl	smile
	wife	wife / wīf	wife
	nice	nise / nīs	nice

Running

White	tired (tīrd)	race (rase)	husband (huz bund)
while	retired (rē tīrd)	been (bin)	breakfast (brek fust)
	every (ev er y)		sometimes (some times)

Fran White is retired. Fran has been retired for three years. Her husband Mike has been retired for five years. These days, the Whites have a lot of time. The Whites have time to do things that they like.

Fran likes to run. Every day, she gets up at five and runs. She is getting ready for a big race. It is a mile race for retired women.

Fran must run five miles every day. Then she will not get tired in the mile race.

Fran has been running every day for three years. Her doctor said that it was OK. At first, Fran did not run very far or very fast. Every week, she ran a little more.

Sometimes, Fran runs in the park. Sometimes, she runs in the street. Today, Fran is running in the park. It is a nice day. People in the park smile at Fran. Fran smiles back at them.

While his wife runs, Mike makes breakfast. He likes to make breakfast while his wife is not in the kitchen.

When Fran comes back, breakfast is ready. Her husband smiles and says, "Is it a nice day?"

"Yes," says his wife. "It is a very nice day."

While they are eating, Mike looks at his wife. "Are you tired, dear?" he asks. "Sometimes, you get very tired."

"Well, I didn't get tired today," Fran says to her husband. "And I am getting fast. I think I am ready for the mile race."

Story Checkup

Circle the letter of the right answer.

1. What does Fran do every day when she gets up?
   a. run
   b. makes breakfast
   c. goes for a drive

2. What is Fran getting ready for?
   a. the five-mile race
   b. the one-mile race
   c. the driving test

3. What time does Fran get up?
   a. at six
   b. at five
   c. at seven

4. What does Mike do while his wife runs?
   a. runs with her
   b. goes to work
   c. makes breakfast

price (prise)	bus
sign (sīn)	age (aje)

In some places, retired people can get things for cheaper prices. At the age of 62 or 65, you can get these cheaper prices. You can ride the bus cheaper. You can get glasses cheaper. You can get many other things cheaper.

To get these cheaper prices, you need a permit. To get a permit, you have to fill in an application.

Here is an application for a bus permit. Fill it in for Mike White. He lives at 1400 Third Street in Dallas, Texas. His zip code is 75210. His date of birth is April 12, 1925. Do not sign your name. Sign his name. Give his age.

City Bus
Application for Retired Person's Permit

_____
Last Name   First Name

Address: _____
         Number and Street

_____
City   State   Zip Code

Date of
Birth: _____ Age: _____ Sex: ☐M ☐F
       Month   Day   Year

_____
Sign Here

Say the words. Circle the words with the sound ī.

1. Miller   mile   wife   with
2. Mike   milk   Smith   smile
3. while   will   tired   third
4. neck   nice   like   lift
5. price   white   pick   which

Copy the word. Add -d or -ed.
Then write one of the words in each sentence.

retire _____   sign _____

smile _____   like _____

1. Fran has been _____ for three years.

2. Mike _____ at his wife.

3. Mike _____ the application.

4. Fran _____ to run in the park.

Drop the -e and add -ing. Write the word.

1. smile _____   4. drive _____

2. retire _____   5. ride _____

3. like _____

Write short answers.

1. What is Fran's last name? _____

2. What is her husband's first name? _____

3. Did the doctor say that it was OK for Fran to run? _____

4. Did Fran run very far at first? _____

5. What does Mike make while Fran runs? _____

6. Does Fran sometimes get tired from running? _____

7. Does Mike run with Fran? _____

8. Does Fran think that she is ready for the mile race? _____

Say the word. Write the number of syllables.

1. sometimes _____   6. nice   _____

2. every   _____   7. cheaper _____

3. breakfast _____   8. permit   _____

4. age   _____   9. husband _____

5. today   _____   10. race   _____

Lesson 13

my = mī
y̅ = ī

y̅ = ī
ie = ī

tie = tī
ie = ī

	cry cried	crȳ cried	cry cried
	dry dried	drȳ dried	dry dried
	try tried	trȳ tried	try tried
	fly	flȳ	fly
	die	die	die

A Brother Dies

by	feel	line
why	air	o'clock (u clock)

One day, Mike got up to make breakfast. It was time for Fran to run, but she was not running. She was sitting next to the telephone. She was crying. Fran tried to dry her eyes when Mike came in.

"Why have you been crying?" Mike asked.

"My brother Tom has died," said Fran. "His wife just telephoned me. She said that he died in his sleep." Fran started to cry again.

Mike tried to make Fran feel better. "There, there, dear," he said. "Cry. You will feel better if you cry."

"He was just 55," Fran cried. "Why did he have to die? Why?"

"Try to think of the happy times that you had with him," said Mike. "Then you will feel better."

Fran cried and cried. Then she dried her eyes. "Ellen will need us," she said. "We must fly there today if we can. I'll start packing while you telephone the air line."

Mike telephoned the air line. "The air line says that we can fly at half past nine," he said to Fran. "We must be there by nine o'clock. Can we be there by nine?"

"We can be ready if we hurry." Fran said. "Tell the air line that we will be there by nine o'clock."

Fran started packing. "Where is your black tie?" she asked Mike. "You will need that tie."

"Here is my black tie," Mike said. "Let me help you. We will save time if I help you."

The Whites packed their bags. From time to time, Fran stopped to dry her eyes. But she and Mike were ready to fly by nine o'clock.

Story Checkup

Answer with the name of a person in the story.

1. Who died in his sleep? _____

2. Who telephoned Fran? _____

3. Who was Ellen? _____

4. Who was Tom's sister? _____

5. Who was Fran's husband? _____

6. Who was Mike's wife? _____

Read these six sentences.
What happened first? You will see a number 1 next to that sentence.
What happened next? Put a number 2 next to that sentence.
Put the right numbers next to the other sentences.

_____ Fran answered the telephone.

_____ Ellen telephoned to Fran.

_____ Mike got up to make breakfast.

___I___ Tom died in his sleep.

_____ The Whites were ready to fly by nine.

_____ Mike telephoned the air line.

a.m.	Monday (Mun day)	service (ser vis)
p.m.	Friday (Frī day)	

When Fran's brother died, this story was in the *King City Times*. Read the story, and write short answers.

King City Times, Friday, April 12, 1996

Tom J. Roberts

Tom J. Roberts, 55, of 162 Green Street, died at 4:00 a.m. today. He died in his sleep at his apartment.

Mr. Roberts worked at the Hill Bicycle Shop for 25 years.

He left his wife, Mrs. Ellen Smith Roberts; two sons, Sam of Bell Gardens and John of Apple Valley; and one sister, Fran Roberts White of Dallas, Texas.

Services will be Monday at 2:30 p.m. at the Little Church in the Valley.

---

1. Who died? _____

2. Where did he live? _____

3. Mr. Roberts died on Friday. What was the date? _____

4. What time on Friday did he die? _____

5. Where did he work? _____

6. Who is his wife? _____

7. Who are his sons? _____

8. Who is the dead man's sister? _____

9. Where does she live? _____

10. What time are the church services on Monday? _____

11. What will the date be on Monday? _____

12. Where will the services be? _____

Practice

Say the words. Circle the words with the sound ī.

1.	cry	city	by	baby
2.	my	dry	play	windy
3.	any	try	eye	tie
4.	puppy	die	why	way
5.	cried	angry	line	nine

**Read the word. Change the y to *i*, and add *-es*.
Write the *-es* word in List 1.**

**Read the word again. Change the y to *i*, and add *-ed*.
Write the *-ed* word in List 2.**

	List 1	List 2
cry	cries	cried
1. dry	_____	_____
2. try	_____	_____
3. carry	_____	_____
4. hurry	_____	_____
5. marry	_____	_____

Fill in the missing word or number.

1. _____ got up to make breakfast.

2. Tom was just _____ when he died.

3. Tom died in his _____.

4. Mike will need his black _____.

5. The Whites were ready by _____ o'clock.

Drop -ing, -d, or -ed. Write the word that is left.

trying ___try___

1. crying	_____	5. died	_____
2. flying	_____	6. tied	_____
3. drying	_____	7. started	_____
4. packing	_____	8. telephoned	_____

igh = ī

night = nīt

igh = ī

	high	high	high
	light	light	light
	flight	flight	flight
	right	right	right
	bright	bright	bright
	sight	sight	sight

A Night Flight from China

find (fīnd)	child (chīld)	I'm (Īm)	sky
behind (bē hīnd)	China (Chī nu)		sad

My name is Lee Chan. I am on a night flight. I'm high in the sky. The night is dark. But the bright lights of my city are still in sight. The bright lights of China are still in sight.

I am going far away, and I feel sad. I'm on a night flight from China to the States. I'm going to the States to study.

From high in the sky, I look for the bright lights again. But they are not in sight. My city is far behind me.

I think of my family that I left behind. I left my wife and my child behind. I will not see them for four years. My child will be five by then. A child needs a father, but I will not be there. Am I doing the right thing?

What will I find in the States? Will I find a place to live? Will I find friends? Am I doing the right thing?

I must not think like that. It makes me sad. I *am* doing the right thing. I'll be OK in the States. I will study very hard. When I go back to China, I'll have a better job. I can take care of my family better. I can help China. I can make things better for my child and other children.

I will not be sad any more. From high in the sky, I see a bright light again. This time, it is the sun. Day has come.

Answer each question with a sentence.

1. Where is Lee Chan from?

   _____

2. Where is he going?

   _____

3. Why is he going there?

   _____

Lee asks himself some questions.
Write four questions that Lee asks himself.

1. _____

2. _____

3. _____

4. _____

| gate | arrive (u rive) | cities (sit yz) |
| | depart (dē part) | timetable (time table) |

Lee Chan has arrived in the States. He has to take another flight to Dallas, Texas. He will take a flight on Sun Air Line.

Here is the Sun Air Line timetable. The timetable has flights to and from many cities on it. On the left are flights that arrive from other cities. On the right are flights that go to other cities.

Study the timetable, and write the answers. When you tell the time, put *a.m.* or *p.m.* in the answer.

SUN AIR LINE

ARRIVE				DEPART			
Flight	**From**		**Gate**	**Flight**	**To**		**Gate**
740	Garden City	8:55 a.m.	2	740	Apple Valley	9:25 a.m.	2
406	Apple Valley	10:00 a.m.	5	406	Dallas	10:30 a.m.	5
505	Little Rock	12:40 p.m.	7	505	Sun Valley	1:20 p.m.	7
419	Dallas	2:00 p.m.	7	670	Dallas	2:40 p.m.	7
680	Sun Valley	2:45 p.m.	4	530	Little Rock	3:15 p.m.	4

1. What time does Flight 740 arrive from Garden City? _____

2. What time does Flight 740 depart for Apple Valley? _____

   If you take this flight, which gate will you go to? _____

3. Two flights go to Dallas. Write the flight numbers. _____

4. Which flight to Dallas departs at 10:30 a.m.? _____

5. Which flight to Dallas departs at 2:40 p.m.? _____

6. Lee will take Flight 670. Which gate will he go to? _____

Practice

Read the sentence. Underline each word with the sound ī.

<u>I</u> am on a <u>night</u> <u>flight</u>.

1. I left my wife and child behind.

2. My child will be five by then.

3. Am I doing the right thing?

4. I must not think like that.

5. The bright lights of China are still in sight.

Sometimes, two little words make one big word. Read the big word. Then write the two little words.

payday	_pay_	_day_
1. himself	_____	_____
2. yourself	_____	_____
3. something	_____	_____
4. sometimes	_____	_____
5. timetable	_____	_____
6. underline	_____	_____

Write three other words with _igh_ that have the sound ī.

high   _____   _____   _____

Write three other words with y that have the sound ī.

by   _____   _____   _____

Write three other words with _i—e_ that have the sound ī.

time   _____   _____   _____

Change the y to _i_, and add -es.
Write one of the words in each sentence.

party   _____   baby   _____

city   _____   story   _____

factory   _____   family   _____

1. I like to read funny _____ .

2. My class had two _____ this year.

3. The _____ are crying.

4. There are flights to many _____ .

5. Many _____ live on this street.

6. The people in the _____ work hard.

More Reading with ā, ē, ī

paper	cake	paint		day
ā	a–e	ai		ay
we	Pete	eat	see	key
ē	e–e	ea	ee	ey
I	time	tie	night	my
ī	i–e	ie	igh	y

1. A Teenager Learns to Drive

_____

learn (lern)

_____

On the day that Jill was 16, she went to the state office building. She filled in an application for a driver's permit. She had to take a written test. The person that gave her the eye test said, "You must have your glasses on when you drive."

Jill got a driver's permit. Her mother started teaching her to drive. Jill learned to make left and right turns. She learned to watch for stop signs and red lights. She learned to watch for other traffic signs while she was driving. She learned to back up and to park.

"I'm ready to try the driving test," said Jill. But she did not pass the test the first time. The tester said that Jill did not stop at a stop sign. She had to take the driving test again. The second time, she passed. "I did it!" said Jill. "I have my driver's license!"

2. A Letter from Ellen Roberts

fine	wives (wīvz)	ago	(u gō)
life	myself (my self)	stories (stor yz)

April 22

Dear Jane,

I have something sad to tell you. My husband Tom died in his sleep ten days ago. That was Friday, April 12.

I was Tom's wife for twenty-nine years. He was a fine husband. We had a happy life.

When Tom died, I telephoned his sister Fran right away. She and her husband Mike arrived from Texas that night. My two sons, Sam and John, came with their wives. The family helped me plan the services.

I liked the services. Tom looked very nice. Many friends were at the church. Tom's family and my family were there. I cried, and they cried with me. It was a sad time, but the services helped me.

After the services, my sons and their wives were standing with me. Friends stopped to say nice things. They said that Tom was a fine man. We cried some more.

My family and I left the church and went back to the apartment. Friends came with many things to eat. We ate and we listened to family stories. My sons heard some of the stories for the first time. We cried and we laughed at these stories.

The services were on Monday, April 15. That was a week ago. My sons and their wives left that night. Fran and Mike left two days ago. I am by myself for the first time.

Things happened very fast. One day, Tom was feeling fine. The next day, he was dead. I can still see his bright smile. I can still see the love in his eyes. Why did he have to die?

I will never stop thinking of Tom. But I must start thinking of myself. I have never lived by myself in my life. I have never had a job in my life. At 49, I must start my life again. I will dry my eyes and do my best.

This letter to you has helped me. I feel a little better. Jane, you are a dear friend.

Love,
Ellen

3. Studying in the States

---

buy (by)   I.D.   English (Ing glish)

Lee Chan has been in the States for two months. He is studying in Dallas, Texas.

The first week that he was there, Lee had a lot to do. He had to find a place to live. He had to buy many things. He had to sign up for classes. He had to get an I.D. card. He had to get a picture for his I.D. card.

Lee had to fill in many applications. Each application asked for his name, address, age, date of birth, place of birth, and sex. Lee got tired of filling in applications. He got tired of standing in line. But, at last, he was ready to start classes.

Lee has been going to class for five weeks. He has been studying very hard. His English is getting much better.

Lee's classes are three miles from where he lives. He had to buy a bicycle. Sometimes, he rides his bicycle to class. Sometimes, he takes the bus.

Lee misses his wife and child in China. But he is making many friends in the States. Two of his friends are Fran and Mike White. The Whites helped Lee find a place to live. They helped him find a bicycle to buy. They are helping him learn English. Lee visits the Whites every Saturday.

Lee likes his life in the States. He likes his classes. He is learning English very well. Lee thinks that prices in the States are high. But he thinks that the people are nice.

4. The Mile Race

---

as (az)   finish (fin ish)   that's

It was the day of the mile race. Fran White ate breakfast, but she didn't eat lunch. "If I eat lunch, I cannot run fast in the race," she said.

Fran's husband Mike went to the race with her. It was a nice day. The sky was bright, and the air was dry. Retired women from five cities were there for the race.

The race started at two o'clock. There were fifteen women in the race. They were at the starting line. When they heard the gun, they started running.

At first, Fran was far behind. She tried harder, and she ran faster. One by one, Fran passed thirteen women. One woman was still running next to Fran. "If I run faster, I can pass her," Fran was thinking. "But I'm running as fast as I can."

The finish line was in sight. Fran ran fast, but the other woman ran as fast as Fran. The two women passed the finish line. It was a tie!

"Nice work!" Mike said to his wife. "You were flying when you passed the finish line. A tie is just fine!"

Fran dried her face and smiled. "That's right!" she said. "It's better to be first, but a tie is not bad."

Ō

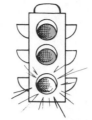

go

ō

	open	ōpen	open
	broken	brōken	broken
	stolen	stōlen	stolen
	sofa	sōfu	sofa
	old	ōld	old
	told	tōld	told

The Door Was Open

Tony (Tō ny)	oh (ō)	door (dor)	we'll (wēl)	someone (some one)
Romano (Rō mon ō)	so (sō)	both (bōth)	police (pu lēs)	anyone (any one)
		gold (gōld)	officer (of is er)	

Tony Romano lived in a big apartment building. One evening after work, Tony got back to his apartment very late. The door was open, and the lock was broken.

"Oh, no!" Tony said. "Someone has broken into my apartment. I'll go next door and telephone the police."

Tony told the police, "My name is Tony Romano. I live at 118 Valley Drive, Apartment 10-B. Someone has broken into my apartment. The door was open when I arrived from work. The door was open, and the lock was broken. I cannot tell if anyone is in there, so I didn't go in. I am telephoning from next door."

"You did the right thing," said the police officer. "We'll send a car right away."

Two police officers arrived very quickly. Both of them had guns. One officer went into Tony's apartment. The other one stayed at the door. They didn't find anyone, so both officers went next door to get Tony.

"Are you Tony Romano?" one officer asked.

"Yes, I am," Tony said. "Did you find anyone?"

"No one was there when I went in," said the other officer. "But someone has been there. Let's go and see what was stolen."

"Oh, my sofa!" said Tony. "My sofa was stolen! It was a gold sofa, and it wasn't very old." Tony looked here and there. "Both my color TV and my clock radio were stolen," he said.

Tony looked some more. "An old gold ring is missing," he told the police. "It was an old gold wedding ring. It was my mother's, so I loved it."

"Is any money missing?" asked one officer.

"Just ten dollars," Tony told her. "I never have much money in the apartment. But will I ever get my things back?"

"We'll work on it," said the police officer. "We'll see if anyone in the building can help us."

After the police left, Tony fixed his lock and went to bed. "I'm happy that my bed wasn't stolen," he said.

Story Checkup

Write Tony's story in four or five sentences.

_____

_____

_____

_____

_____

_____

_____

_____

sale

After Tony Romano's sofa was stolen, he needed another one. Tony didn't have much money, so he looked at ads in the paper. He looked for an old sofa.

These are the ads that Tony looked at. Read them, and write short answers to the questions.

FOR SALE

Green sofa with matching chair. 2 years old. $350 for both. 472-1653 after 5.

Kitchen table and four chairs, painted white. Very nice. $50. 946 Second Street. Must sell this week.

Apartment sale: sofa, coffee table, large rug, chairs, dishes, pans. 205 Valley Drive. Saturday, 9 a.m. to 4 p.m.

FOR SALE

Gold sofa—$75, green curtains—$15, bed—$40, black and white TV—$30, 2 radios—$10 each, wedding dress—$75, tent—$20. 422-9121 any time.

Old clocks, dolls, glass plates, picture frames, quart jars. Old Red Barn, 3267 River Street. Open every day from 10 a.m. to 6 p.m.

Color TV—$140, gray sofa—cost $800, will sell for $400. 476-3986.

1. Are the green sofa and chair three years old? _____

   What is the price of both? _____

   What is the telephone number? _____

2. What day is the apartment sale? _____

   Does the ad tell the price of this sofa? _____

   What is the address? _____

3. What is the price of the gold sofa? _____

4. What is the price of the gray sofa? _____

5. Which is cheaper, the gray sofa or the gold one? _____

6. Which is cheaper, the gold sofa or the green sofa and chair? _____

Read the sentence. Underline each word with the sound ō.

1. The door was open, and the lock was broken.

2. Both my clock radio and my color TV were stolen.

3. Tony's sofa was stolen.

4. An old gold ring is missing.

5. Let's go and see what was stolen.

Read the word. Write the two words that it comes from.

I'll   <u> I </u>   <u> will </u>

1. that's   _____   _____

2. we'll   _____   _____

3. didn't   _____   _____

4. I'm   _____   _____

Fill in the right word: we'll, I'm, that's, didn't.

1. _____ a nice sofa.

2. _____ see you at the party.

3. _____ tired of standing in line.

4. Tony _____ go into his apartment by himself.

Answer each question with a sentence.

1. Did Tony Romano live in a big apartment building or a little one?

_____

2. What was broken at Tony's apartment?

_____

3. Where did Tony go to telephone the police?

_____

4. Why did Tony love the gold ring that was stolen?

_____

Say the word. Write the number of syllables.

1. someone _____   6. telephone _____

2. police _____   7. arrived _____

3. officer _____   8. quickly _____

4. broken _____   9. sale _____

5. sofa _____   10. missing _____

Lesson 17

$$o - e = \bar{o}$$

home = hōm

$$o - e = \bar{o}$$

	robe	robe rōb	robe
	nose	noze nōz	nose
	woke	woke wōk	woke
	smoke	smoke smōk	smoke
	phone	fone fōn	phone
	alone	u lone u lōn	alone

A Fire at Home

Rose (Rōze)	Joe (Jō)	smell	department (dē part ment)
Stone	cold (cōld)	fire	cigarette (sig u ret)
hope		glad	

It was late at night. Joe Stone was home alone. He had on his robe. He was smoking in bed while he watched TV. Joe never smoked in bed while his wife, Rose, was home. But he sometimes smoked in bed when he was alone.

Joe went to sleep with his cigarette in his hand. The cigarette didn't burn Joe's robe, but it did burn the bed covers. Smoke filled the air.

Joe was sleeping, so he did not smell the smoke. But Joe's puppy smelled the smoke. The puppy jumped on the bed and put its cold nose on Joe's face. The puppy's cold nose woke Joe up.

When Joe woke up, the bed was on fire. "I must phone the fire department, but not from here," he said. "I'll go next door to phone." Joe picked up the puppy and ran into the cold night. He ran next door and phoned the fire department.

The fire department worked fast. A fire truck arrived at Joe's home very quickly. Joe was standing in the street.

Men and women came on the fire truck. "Is anyone in there?" one of them asked Joe.

"No," Joe answered. "I was home alone. I'm glad that you are here. I hope that you can save my home."

The men and women started putting water on the fire. Joe watched them with the puppy in his arms. It was cold, so Joe put the puppy in his robe.

Rose Stone came home while the fire was burning. She ran to her husband. "Oh, Joe!" she said. "I'm glad that you are OK. We worked very hard to buy this home. I hope that they can save it."

Rose picked up the puppy and patted its nose. "I'm glad that you saved the puppy," she said.

"I didn't save him," said Joe. "He saved me. He smelled the smoke and woke me up. I was smoking in bed, but I have learned my lesson."

"I hope so," said Rose.

The people from the fire department saved the Stones' home. The Stones thanked the men and women for saving their home.

Story Checkup

Read these eight sentences.
What happened first? Put a number 1 by that sentence.
Put the right numbers by the other sentences.

_____ Joe went to sleep.

_____ Joe phoned the fire department.

_____ Joe was smoking in bed.

_____ Rose Stone came home.

_____ The cigarette burned the covers.

_____ The puppy smelled the smoke.

_____ A fire truck arrived at Joe's home.

_____ The puppy woke up Joe.

don't (dōnt) anything (any thing) everyone (every one)

Phoning for help

Keep the numbers of the police and fire department by your telephone. If you need help, you can find the phone number quickly.

What do you say when you phone the fire department?

1. Give your name.
2. Give your street address.
   Add anything that will help them find you.
3. Tell what has happened.
4. Give the other person time to ask you more.

What Joe said on the phone

This is what Joe Stone told the fire department when he phoned. Did Joe say the right things?

Joe Stone: This is Joe Stone. There is a fire in my home. It's at 1428 Garden Drive. That's not far from Second Street. The fire started in a bed at the back of the building.

Fire department: Where are you?

Joe Stone: I'm phoning from next door.

Fire department: Is everyone away from the building?

Joe Stone: Yes, I was home alone.

Fire department: Fine. Don't go back home. Don't try to save anything.

If you have a fire

Here are some other things to think of if you have a fire.

1. Get everyone away from the burning building fast.
   Don't stop to telephone. Don't stop to take anything with you.
2. Phone the fire department from next door or from a pay phone.
3. Never go back into a burning building.

Read the sentences. Underline each word with the sound ō.

1. Joe Stone was home alone.

2. Joe was smoking in bed.

3. The puppy's cold nose woke up Joe.

4. I hope that you can save my home.

5. Joe put the puppy in his robe.

6. I will not phone from here.

Read the big word. Then write the two little words that you see in it.

anything   _any_   _thing_

1. someone   _____   _____

2. anyone   _____   _____

3. everyone   _____   _____

4. myself   _____   _____

5. himself   _____   _____

6. yourself   _____   _____

Write a short *yes* or *no* answer.

1. Was Joe home alone? _____

2. Did the cigarette burn Joe's robe? _____

3. Did Joe phone from his home? _____

4. Did the puppy save Joe's life? _____

5. Did the fire department save the Stones' home? _____

Read each word. In List 1, write the word with *-ing*.
In List 2, write the word with *-d* or *-ed*.

	List 1	**List 2**
smoke	Smoking	Smoked
1. phone	_____	_____
2. save	_____	_____
3. smell	_____	_____
4. arrive	_____	_____
5. answer	_____	_____

oa = ō

boat = bōt

oa = ō

	coat	coat	coat
	road	road	road
	load	load	load
	loaf	loaf	loaf
	toast	toast	toast
	roast	roast	roast

Camping in October

Joan	lake	camp		shore	(shor)	over (ō ver)
rain	made	end		clothes	(clōz)	October (Oc tō ber)
Oak		weekend (week end)		wear	(wār)	heavy (hev y)

"Let's go camping this weekend," said Joan to her mother. "There is a state park at Green Lake. It's on Shore Road. We can rent a boat there."

"Fine," said Mrs. Oak. "I think that camping in October is fun. What shall we take to eat? Let's see, we'll need coffee, apples, cheese, eggs, and a loaf of bread. Shall we take any meat?"

"No, we'll go fishing," Joan told her mother."We can roast fish over a fire. Wear old clothes, and bring a heavy coat. It's cold at the lake in October, and sometimes it rains."

On Saturday, Joan and her mother loaded the back end of their truck. They loaded their tent and two sleeping bags into the truck. They loaded other things that they needed.

Mrs. Oak and Joan were on the road by seven o'clock. Mrs. Oak was wearing old clothes and her husband's heavy hunting coat. Joan was wearing old clothes and a heavy coat.

They got to Shore Road at eight o'clock. The state park was at the end of the road. After they put up their tent, Mrs. Oak went to rent a boat. Joan cut the loaf of bread and made cheese sandwiches.

The two women spent the day fishing on the lake. At the end of the day, they each had six fish.

When they got to the shore, Mrs. Oak made a fire and Joan cleaned the fish. Joan roasted the fish over the fire. While Joan was roasting the fish, Mrs. Oak made coffee and toast. She cut some bread from the loaf and toasted it over the fire.

After dinner, they watched the fire for a while. Then they got into their sleeping bags and went to sleep.

The next day, it rained for a while. After it stopped raining, the two women fished again. Then they went for a boat ride on the lake.

"This has been a nice weekend," said Joan. "Let's go camping again when Dad is home. Do you think that you and Dad can go next weekend?"

"Yes, I think so," said Mrs. Oak. "Your dad will like camping at this lake in October."

Story Checkup

Write short answers.

1. What month was it? _____

2. Where did Joan and her mother go camping?

   _____

3. What did they take with them to eat? _____

   _____

4. What other things did they take? _____

   _____

5. Why did they rent a boat? _____

map   way

ROAD MAP

King City

Green Lake
State Park

Green Lake

Shore-Road

Center-Road

Valley-Road

Center-Road

Mud Lake

Apple Valley

Stone-Hill-Road

Write the answers. Find the answers by looking at the road map.

1. What road goes from King City to Apple Valley?

   _____

2. What is the best road to take from Apple Valley to Mud Lake?

   _____

3. The Oaks live in King City. Which roads do they take to the state park?

   _____   _____

   _____

Circle the right answers. Find the answers by looking at the map.

1. Mrs. Oak and Joan are on their way to the state park. They are on Center Road. When they get to Valley Road, which way do they turn?   Left   Right

2. They are on Valley Road. When they get to Shore Road, which way do they turn?   Left   Right

Say the words. Circle the words with the sound ō.

1. Joan   John   Joe   Jason
2. red   road   Rosa   robe
3. bat   boat   both   box
4. cold   cop   coat   come
5. top   toast   roast   best
6. left   love   load   loaf

Copy the word. Add the ending -y. Make a change in the word if you have to. Write one of the words in each sentence.

wind   _windy_   fun   _funny_

rain _____   sun _____

sleep _____   rock _____

1. It's fun to be at the shore on a _____ day.

2. It's not fun to be there on a _____ day.

3. Carla put her _____ child to bed.

4. Joan does not like to run on the _____ path.

Answer with the name of a person in the story.

1. Who went to rent a boat? _____

2. Who made cheese sandwiches? _____

3. Who cleaned the fish? _____

4. Who roasted the fish? _____

5. Who made coffee and toast? _____

Read the big word. Then write the two little words that you see in it.

anyone ___any___ ___one___

1. weekend _____ _____

2. everyone _____ _____

3. homework _____ _____

4. cannot _____ _____

5. someone _____ _____

6. anything _____ _____

7. yourself _____ _____

$\overline{O}W = \overline{O}$

snow = snō

$\overline{o}w = \overline{o}$

	blow	blōw	blow
	show	shōw	show
	know	nōw	know
	throw	thrōw	throw
	window	win dōw	window
	follow	fol ōw	follow

Stuck in the Snow

slowly (slōw ly)	below (bē lōw)	wind	side	you're (your)
yellow (yel ōw)	zero (zē rō)	sand	ice (ise)	onto (on to)
				ahead (u head)

It is snowing, and the wind is blowing. It is five below zero. The wind is blowing so hard that it feels much colder. It feels like forty below zero. There is snow and ice on the road.

Sam is on his way home from hockey practice. He is driving his father's car. Sam knows that he must drive slowly in the snow. It is snowing so hard that Sam cannot see the road. He follows the lights of the car ahead of him.

The wind blows snow onto Sam's car windows. Sam stops by the side of the road. He cleans the snow and ice from his windows.

A yellow car passes Sam. It is not going slowly. The yellow car throws more ice and snow onto Sam's windows.

Sam cleans his windows again. "He is driving very fast," Sam thinks. "He is going so fast that he will miss the turn up ahead."

Sam gets back in his car and drives slowly. When he comes to the turn in the road, he sees the yellow car again. It is on the side of the road. It is stuck in the snow and ice. Sam stops to help the driver.

The man says, "I'm stuck, and I don't know what to do."

"I have a bag of sand in my car," says Sam. "I'll throw some sand under your wheels." Sam throws sand under the wheels of the car.

Then Sam tells the man to rock the car. "Drive ahead a little. Then drive back," he says. "Then drive ahead a little more. Make a path in the snow." But the man does not know what to do.

"Here, let me show you," Sam says. He gets into the man's car on the driver's side. Sam shows him what to do. Sam rocks the car and gets it onto the road again.

The man says, "You're not very old, but you know a lot. Thanks for showing me. If this ever happens again, I'll know what to do."

Sam says, "It's no fun to get stuck when it's below zero. I was glad to help you. If you're going my way, you can follow me. Follow the lights of my car."

Story Checkup

Write the story in three or four sentences.

_____

_____

_____

_____

_____

_____

Read these traffic signs.

speed limit (lim it)

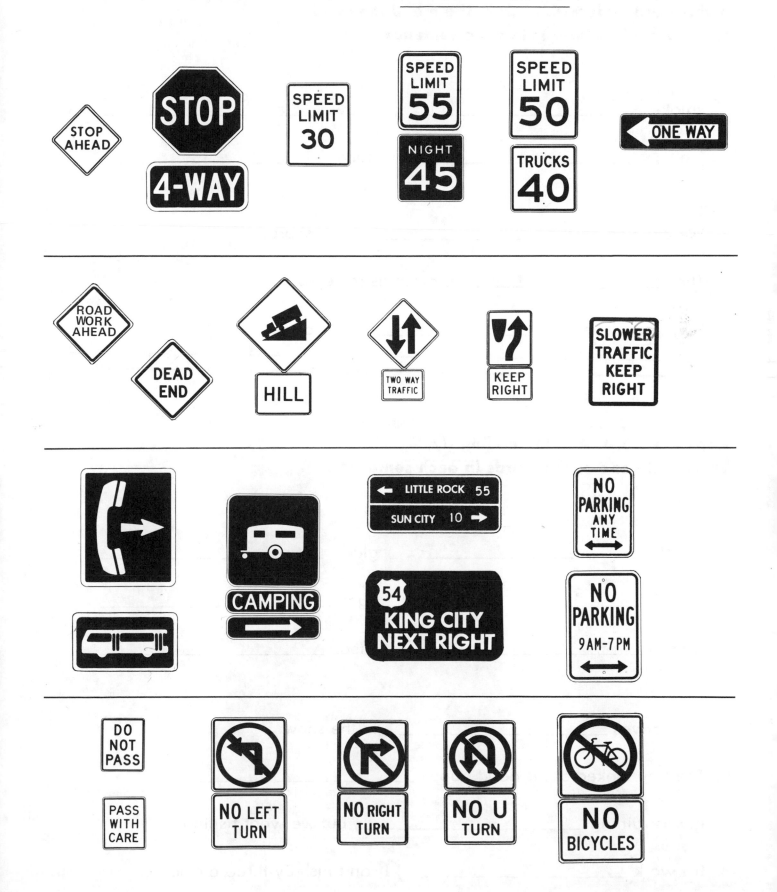

Copy the word. Add the ending -y to each word.
If the word ends with e, drop the e and then add -y.
Write one of the words in each sentence.

smoke _____   snow _____

ice _____   sand _____

1. We camped on the _____ shore.

2. The _____ air hurts my eyes.

3. I will not drive on _____ roads.

Copy the word. Add the ending -ly.
Then write one of the words in each sentence.

quick _____   glad _____

slow _____   light _____

sad _____   cheap _____

1. Sam drives _____ in the snow.

2. The boy looked at his dead puppy _____.

3. It was raining _____, but we went fishing.

4. If I work _____, I can finish by three o'clock.

Write a short yes or no answer.

1. Does Sam drive slowly in the snow? _____

2. Does Sam's car get stuck? _____

3. Is it forty below zero? _____

4. Is Sam on his way to hockey practice? _____

5. Does Sam help the man in the yellow car? _____

6. Does Sam throw sand under the car wheels? _____

Drop the ending from each word. Write the word that is left.
Make a change in the word if you have to.

having ___have___   shopped ___shop___

1. stopped _____   6. rained _____

2. loaded _____   7. quickly _____

3. windy _____   8. slowly _____

4. icy _____   9. sleeping _____

5. smoking _____   10. running _____

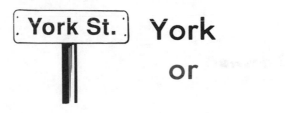 York
or

or

ore = or

 store
ore = or

40	forty	for ty	forty
	short	short	short
	corner	cor ner	corner
	tore	tore	tore
	before	bē fore	before

At the Department Store

wore	fourth (forth)	than	what's
sport	floor (flor)	want (wont)	cheapest (cheap est)
shirt	Porter (Port er)	most (mōst)	salesperson (sales person)
sleeve		close (cloze)	

Steve was hurrying up York Street. He was on his way to Porter's Department Store. Porter's was on the corner of York Street and Fourth Street.

Steve's friend David was at the corner. "What's the hurry?" David asked.

"I have to buy a sport shirt before the store closes," Steve said. "I wore my brother's best sport shirt last night, and I tore it. I tore the sleeve on the car door."

"One time, I wore my father's shirt and tore it," David said. "He's still angry that I wore his shirt."

"I want to buy another shirt like my brother's before he gets home," said Steve. "I'm in a hurry. See you later."

Steve looked at a sign on the first floor. It said that men's clothes were on the fourth floor. Steve hurried up to the fourth floor. He went to the men's department. "I want a yellow shirt with short sleeves," he told the salesperson.

"The shirts with short sleeves are over there," said the salesperson.

Steve picked up a red shirt with short sleeves. It cost fourteen dollars. A green shirt cost twenty dollars. "That one costs more than the red one, but it's a better shirt," said the salesperson. "And this yellow one is Porter's best sport shirt," he added.

Steve was thinking, "The best shirt will cost the most." And he was right. The yellow shirt did cost the most. It cost thirty dollars.

"I have forty dollars," Steve was thinking. "The green shirt is cheaper than the yellow one, and the red shirt is the cheapest. But I will have to buy the one that costs the most. The yellow shirt is like my brother's."

"The store is going to close," the salesperson said. "Do you want to buy anything before it closes?"

"Yes," said Steve, "I'll take the thirty-dollar shirt. Here is forty dollars."

Steve got back some change from his forty dollars. He picked up the shirt and hurried to the corner. On the bus, he was thinking, "It cost me thirty dollars to wear a shirt one time! I'll never wear my brother's clothes again."

Story Checkup

order (or der)

In what order did these things happen?
Put a number by each sentence to show the right order.
If you don't know the order, please read the story again.

_____ Steve was hurrying up York Street.

_____ Steve tore his brother's shirt.

_____ Steve looked at a sign on the first floor.

_____ The salesperson showed Steve the best shirt in the store.

_____ Steve got back some change.

_____ Steve gave the salesperson forty dollars.

& (and)   directory (di rec tor y)

Porter's Department Store			
FIRST FLOOR	**SECOND FLOOR**	**THIRD FLOOR**	**FOURTH FLOOR**

Garden Shop
Bake Shop
Clocks & Watches
Coffee Shop
Paper
	Women's Clothes
	  Skirts, Shirts
	  Dresses, Hats
	
	Children's Department
	  Children's Clothes
	  Baby Clothes
		For the Home
		  Beds
		  Sofas & Chairs
		  Dishes
		  Curtains
		  Radios & TVs
			Men's Department
			  Coats
			  Shirts
			
			Sports Department
			  Bicycles
			  Tents
			  Boats

This is a store directory. A store directory is a sign. It tells where to find things in the store. The directory is on the first floor. Some stores have a directory on every floor.

Look at this store directory, and answer the questions below.

1. On which floor can you find men's coats? _____

2. On which floor can you find a dress for a baby? _____

3. On which floor can you buy a radio? _____

4. On which floor can you get something to eat? _____

5. Where is the sports department? _____

6. Which floor has things for camping? _____

7. In which shop can you get a loaf of bread? _____

8. Which floor has things for the kitchen? _____

Say the words. Circle the words with the sound or.

1. shirt short hurt shore
2. tore wore are fire
3. brother order corner burn
4. sport start floor door
5. turn store wear York

Add -er to each word, and write the -er word in List 1.
Add -est to each word, and write the -est word in List 2.

	List 1	**List 2**
cheap	cheaper	cheapest
1. slow		
2. fast		
3. short		
4. high		
5. light		
6. bright		
7. clean		

Write the missing number word.

first, third, thirty, fourth, fourteen, forty

1. Steve looked at a sign on the _____ floor.

2. He looked at sport shirts on the _____ floor.

3. The cheapest shirt cost _____ dollars.

4. The best shirt cost _____ dollars.

5. Steve gave the salesperson _____ dollars.

Write the missing endings: -ing, -ed, -y, -ly, -er, -est.

1. Sam drives the car very slow_____.

2. Steve looks at three shirts, but he doesn't buy

   the cheap_____ one.

3. Kitty lives in a wind_____ city.

4. Steve was hurry_____ up York Street.

5. Mrs. Oak toast_____ the bread over the fire.

6. I am short_____ than my brother.

More Reading with ā, ē, ī, ō, or

paper	cake	paint		day
ā	a–e	ai		ay
we	Pete	eat	see	key
ē	e–e	ea	ee	ey
I	time	tie	night	my
ī	i–e	ie	igh	y
go	home	boat	snow	
ō	o–e	oa	ōw	
York	store			
or	ore			

1. The Ring That Was Stolen

---

broke   stole

One day in October, a police officer phoned Tony Romano. "This is Officer Roberts," she said. "I came to your home when someone broke into it. We think that two men stole your things. We think that we have both men."

Tony said, "Did you find my old gold ring? I hope so."

The officer told him, "Come to the police department, and we'll show you a ring. We think that it is yours."

Tony asked, "Did you find my sofa and other things?"

The officer said, "No, we don't have them yet. If we find anything, we'll let you know."

After a while, Tony got his gold ring back. But he never got back the other things that were stolen.

2. Joe Quit Smoking

quit	morning (morn ing)
won't (wōnt)	instead (in sted)

The morning after the fire, Joe Stone quit smoking. "I'm throwing my cigarettes away," he said. "I won't start another fire in my home."

His wife Rose was glad. She wanted Joe to live many more years. She didn't like smoke in her eyes and nose. She didn't like the smell of smoke in her clothes.

But it was hard for Joe to quit. "I have been smoking for forty years," he said. "If I quit, I won't have anything to do with my hands."

Every morning, Joe wanted a cigarette when he woke up. But he got up and made toast instead. He wanted to smoke when he was home alone. But he painted his boat instead. Joe wanted a cigarette every night before he went to sleep. But he kissed Rose instead.

One morning, Joe told Rose, "I have not smoked for four months. I won't ever smoke again."

3. The End of a Cold Night

---

forget (for get)   young (yung)   Jones (Jōnz)

When Bob Jones got stuck in the snow and ice, Sam helped him get his car onto the road again. Then Mr. Jones followed Sam's car. At the corner of Oak and Shore Roads, both cars stopped. Sam opened his window and yelled, "I'm turning here. Can you find your way alone? Your brother's home is two miles ahead. It's at the end of the road. Don't forget to drive slowly."

Mr. Jones yelled back, "I won't forget. Thanks a lot. You're a fine young man."

At his brother's home, Mr. Jones told his story. "I was stuck in the snow. The wind was blowing hard, and it was below zero. A young man stopped to help me. I will never forget that young man. He saved my life."

4. A Shirt Story

"Where is my yellow sport shirt?" Tom asked his brother.

Steve said, "I wore it last night, and I tore it on the car door."

"What?" said Tom. "You tore my best shirt! I wanted to wear it tonight."

"Don't be angry," said Steve. "I got you another one at Porter's Department Store. See, it's yellow, and it has short sleeves just like yours. It cost me thirty dollars."

"Oh," said Tom. "I got my shirt on sale. It was cheaper than this one. You're not a bad brother. You can wear my sport coat if you want to."

"No, thanks," said Steve. "I'm going to a party this weekend, but I'll wear my old coat."

Ū

music

Ū

	United States	Ū nīt ed	United States
	Cuba	Cū bu	Cuba
	menu	men ū	menu
	university	Ū ni ver si ty	university
	refugees	ref ū jeez	refugees
	future	f ū cher	future

A Family from Cuba

Hugo (Hū gō)	Garcia (Gar sē u)	studied (stud yd)	speak
Cuban (Cū bun)	citizen (sit i zen)	forward (for werd)	wait
union (ūn yun)	Florida (Flor i du)	became (bē came)	band
			U.S.

Hugo and Rosa Garcia came from Cuba with their three sons. The Garcia family came to the United States with other Cuban refugees.

The Cuban refugees came to the United States for a better future. They looked forward to a better future for their children. They wanted to be United States citizens.

The refugees came from Cuba on a boat. They came to Florida. At first, they lived in a refugee camp.

A family in Union Park, Florida, became friends with the Garcias. They helped the Garcias find a place to live in Union Park. They helped Hugo and Rosa find jobs.

Hugo was a music teacher in Cuba. He wanted to teach in the United States. But he didn't speak English very well. So Hugo got a job in a band. The band played on weekends. In the mornings, he cut grass and cleaned buildings at a university.

Rosa got a job in a snack shop. At first, she didn't know the words on the menu. So she had to work in the kitchen.

The Garcias had to work very hard. But they looked forward to a better future.

Rosa studied the words and prices on the menu. When she learned to read the menu, she got a better job. She waited on tables at the snack shop. Rosa liked to wait on tables. She liked to speak English with the people that came in.

Hugo got into a union. In the union, he got more money than he did before. He played in a bigger band.

The Garcias' sons looked forward to going to a university. They worked part time and saved their money. Later, each of them studied at a university in Florida.

The Garcias had to wait five years before they became U.S. citizens. They became fine citizens.

Story Checkup

Write a short answer to each question.

1. Where did the Garcias live before they came to the United States? _____

2. What state did they come to in the United States?

   _____

3. What city did they live in? _____

4. Where did Rosa work? _____

5. What job did Hugo have on weekends? _____

   _____

country (cun try)	America (U mār i cu)	near
countries (cun tryz)	Mexico (Mex i cō)	north
		biggest (big est)

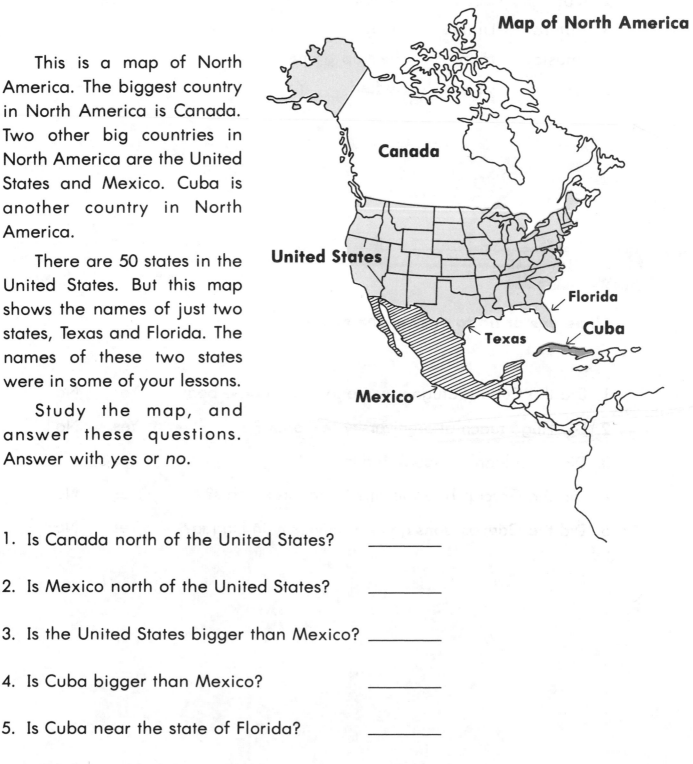

Map of North America

Canada

United States

Florida

Texas

Cuba

Mexico

This is a map of North America. The biggest country in North America is Canada. Two other big countries in North America are the United States and Mexico. Cuba is another country in North America.

There are 50 states in the United States. But this map shows the names of just two states, Texas and Florida. The names of these two states were in some of your lessons.

Study the map, and answer these questions. Answer with *yes* or *no*.

1. Is Canada north of the United States? _____

2. Is Mexico north of the United States? _____

3. Is the United States bigger than Mexico? _____

4. Is Cuba bigger than Mexico? _____

5. Is Cuba near the state of Florida? _____

6. Is Mexico near the state of Texas? _____

Practice

Say the words. Circle the words with the sound ū.

1. Hugo   hunt   union   hurt
2. cut   Cuba   church   Cuban
3. future   United   funny   under
4. music   men   checkup   menu
5. young   you   studied   York

Homework

Circle _yes_ or _no_ to answer the question.

1. Did the Cuban refugees come to Florida on a boat?   Yes   No
2. Did Hugo teach at a university in Florida?   Yes   No
3. Did Rosa learn to speak English?   Yes   No
4. Did the Garcias become citizens in three years?   Yes   No
5. Did the Garcias' sons go to a university in Florida?   Yes   No

A Baby Brings Changes

Tell your answer to each question.

1. What changes in Jason's way of life did the baby bring?
    Which change do you think upset Jason the most?
2. What changes in Gail's way of life did the baby bring?
    Which change do you think upset her the most?
3. Why did Gail want to go back to work after the baby came?
4. Why didn't Jason want Gail to work?
5. What plan did Gail and Jason agree to try?
6. What do you think of their plan?

Write a short answer to each question.

1. What was the baby's name? _____

2. Where did Jason go one Saturday? _____

3. What two things do Gail and Mary plan to share?

_____

Is Love Enough?

Tell your answer to each question.

1. Did Maria like to be a migrant? Why or why not?
2. What did Maria tell Carlos the first time he asked her to marry him?
3. In what ways do you think that love changed Carlos and Maria?
4. Do you like the name of the story?
   What other name can you think of for the story?

Write a short answer to each question.

1. What was one crop that Maria picked? _____

2. Who was the farmer's son? _____

3. Who helped Carlos find a teacher? _____

4. Which man did Maria love? _____

Homework

Read the word. Write the two words that it comes from.

1. we're _____ _____   4. don't _____ _____

2. what's _____ _____   5. won't _____ _____

3. you're _____ _____   6. can't _____ _____

Fill in the right word: we're, can't, won't, what's, don't, you're.

1. "_____ the matter?" asked Jason.

2. "_____ going to be parents," said Gail.

3. "We _____ afford a baby-sitter," said Jason.

4. "I _____ be upset," said Gail to herself.

5. "_____ nice, Carlos," said Maria.

6. "Please, Maria, _____ let Ed come near you," said Carlos.

Helen Keller

Tell your answer to each question.

1. What three handicaps did Helen Keller overcome?
2. Do you think that Anne Sullivan was a good teacher? Why or why not?
3. In what ways did Helen Keller help other handicapped people?
4. Do you like this story? Why or why not?

Write a short answer to each question.

1. When was Helen Keller born? _____

2. Was she blind and deaf from birth? _____

3. What was the first word that Helen was able to understand? _____

4. What kind of writing can many blind people read? _____

Martin Luther King Jr.

Tell your answer to each question.

1. Why did Dr. King and the others start a bus boycott?
   What change did the boycott make for blacks in Montgomery?
2. Why did blacks in Birmingham have sit-ins?
3. What big changes came from civil rights protests in the 1960s?
4. What do you think of Dr. King's way of fighting for civil rights?

Write a short answer to each question.

1. Who led blacks in their fight for civil rights?

_____

2. What prize did he win? _____

3. What was Dr. King's age when he was killed? _____

Word List

Skill Book 3: Long Vowel Sounds introduces the 426 words and 3 symbols listed below. Variants formed by adding -*s, -es, -'s, -s', -ed, -ing,* and -*er* (comparative) to previously taught words are not listed except when *y* is changed to *i* before an ending. New words are listed in their root form when they are used with these previously taught endings. Italics indicate that a word taught earlier as a sight word is reintroduced and taught phonetically in this book.

The correlated reader, *Changes,* introduces additional words. Those words are listed at the back of that book. Lessons to accompany the correlated reader use some of those words, but they are not listed in this book.

Word	Lesson	Word	Lesson	Word	Lesson	Word	Lesson
ad	8	be	7	card	3	cried	13
again	7	beans	8	care	5	cries	13
age	12	became	22	Carla	1	cry	13
ago	15	been	12	¢ (cent)	1	Cuba	22
ahead	19	beer	7	chair	4	Cuban	22
air	13	before	20	*change	13	Dallas	11
alone	17	behind	14	cheap	8	date	5
a.m.	13	below	19	cheapest	20	David	1
America	22	best	8	check	3	day	3
& (and)	20	bicycle	11	cheese	8	dear	5
angry	7	biggest	22	child	14	depart	14
*answer	2	bill	1	China	14	department	17
anyone	16	birth	11	church	5	didn't	7
anything	17	blow	19	cigarette	17	die	13
apartment	2	boat	18	cities	14	directory	20
application	11	both	16	citizen	22	$ (dollar)	1
April	2	breakfast	12	class	1	don't	17
arrive	14	bright	14	clean	9	door	16
as	15	broke	21	close (cloze)	20	dried	13
ate	5	broken	16	clothes	18	drink	1
away	3	bus	12	coat	18	drive	11
baby	2	buy	15	coffee	1	driver	11
baby-sitter	2	by	13	cold	17	dry	13
bake	5	cake	5	corner	20	each	8
baker	8	came	5	cost	1	eat	8
band	22	camp	18	countries	22	eaten	8
bank	3	Canada	10	country	22	eight	7

*Indicates words that are introduced in titles or directions.

Word	Lesson	Word	Lesson	Word	Lesson	Word	Lesson
eighteen	7	Green	7	late	7	need	7
eighty	7	had	3	learn	15	never	4
eleven	7	hair	4	Lee	7	next	3
end	18	ham	1	license	11	nice	12
English	15	hamburger	1	life	15	night	14
evening	9	*he*	7	light	14	nine	7
ever	4	heavy	18	like	12	nineteen	7
every	12	here	9	limit	19	ninety	7
everyone	17	high	14	line	13	north	22
eye	11	*himself	14	*listen*	1	nose	17
face	7	hockey	10	load	18	Oak	18
feel	13	home	17	loaf	18	o'clock	13
fifteen	7	hope	17	Lopez	1	October	18
fifty	7	Hugo	22	love	2	officer	16
find	14	hundred	3	made	18	oh	16
fine	15	husband	12	make	9	OK	4
finish	15	*I*	1	map	18	old	16
fire	17	ice	19	Mason	3	onto	19
flight	14	icy	19	May	3	open	16
floor	20	I.D.	15	me	2	*order	20
Florida	22	if	11	meal	8	over	18
fly	13	I'll	1	meat	8	paid	4
follow	19	I'm	14	menu	22	paint	4
forget	21	instant	2	Mexico	22	paper	1
forty	7	instead	21	Mike	12	part	9
forward	22	it's	7	mile	12	party	5
fourteen	7	Jane	5	milk	1	pat	2
fourth	20	Jason	1	*missing	1	pay	3
frame	5	Joan	18	Monday	13	payday	3
Friday	13	Joe	17	money	9	people	8
future	22	Jones	21	month	2	permit	11
Gail	4	Kay	3	*more	6	Pete	9
gallon	4	keep	9	morning	21	phone	17
Garcia	22	key	9	most	20	place	9
gate	14	know	19	much	5	plate	5
gave	5	labor	9	music	1	play	3
glad	17	lady	2	*my*	1	player	10
go	1	lake	18	myself	15	please	8
gold	16	landlady	4	nail	4	p.m.	13
gray	4	last	3	near	22	police	16

Word	Lesson	Word	Lesson	Word	Lesson	Word	Lesson
Porter	20	shall	4	*study*	1	wait	22
potatoes	2	shirt	20	*syllable	2	want	20
*practice	2	shore	18	table	2	wasn't	7
price	12	*short	3	take	5	water	2
quart	4	show	19	tax	9	way	18
*question	14	side	19	tea	8	we	1
quit	21	sight	14	teach	9	wear	18
race	12	sign	12	teacher	8	wedding	5
radio	2	sixteen	7	team	10	week	9
rain	18	sixty	7	teenager	10	weekend	18
Ray	3	sky	14	teeth	7	we'll	16
*read	1	sleep	7	test	11	what's	20
reader	8	sleeve	20	tester	11	wheel	7
refugee	22	slow	19	Texas	11	where	5
rent	3	slowly	19	than	20	while	12
repair	9	smell	17	that's	15	White	12
retired	12	smile	12	there	5	why	13
ride	11	smoke	17	these	9	wife	12
*right	5	snack	1	third	9	wind	19
road	18	snow	19	thirteen	7	window	19
roast	18	so	16	thirty	7	wives	15
robe	17	sofa	16	throw	19	woke	17
Romano	16	someone	16	tie	13	won't	21
Rosa	2	something	8	time	11	wore	20
Rose	17	sometimes	12	timetable	14	*write*	1
sad	14	*sound	2	tired	12	writer	8
salad	1	speak	22	toast	18	written	11
sale	16	speed	19	today	3	year	10
salesperson	20	spent	3	told	16	yellow	19
same	11	sport	20	Tony	16	yesterday	3
sand	19	stairs	4	tore	20	yet	5
sandwich	1	state	11	tree	7	*York*	1
Saturday	9	Steve	9	tried	13	young	21
save	9	still	5	try	13	your	3
*say	2	stole	21	TV	6	you're	19
second	9	stolen	16	*underline	14	yourself	5
see	7	Stone	17	union	22	zero	19
sentence	1	store	20	United States	22	zip code	11
service	13	stories	15	university	22		
seventeen	7	*story	1	U.S.	22		
sex	11	studied	22	*valley*	9		